THE
ILLUSTRATED
JOURNEY
TO THE
CENTER
OF THE
WHOLE

A Path To Self-Mastery

Richard S. Omura

www.RichardOmura.com

Conceived, written, designed and crafted by
Richard S. Omura

Photography by Richard S. Omura
All Rights Reserved (C)

2

Other books by Richard S. Omura

The Tao of God
The Seven Circles
Katsugen—The Gentle Art of Well Being
The Whole Universe Book
Alien Angels
The Self-Creating Consciousness

There is no Out

without the In.

There is no Whole

Without the Part.   3

This is where we start...

Just a human-like animal...

4

Eating,
    sleeping,
        defecating,
            reproducing,

    doing the animal things
        we need to do...

We've all been at this stage...
Human, but very animalistic...
Foolish but realistic.

Using human ingenuity
for animal purposes.
Giving humanity a bad name...

Most of us are here...
Enduring strife...
indecisive...uncertain
on the big questions of life:
death, purpose and destiny.

Just living, just existing,
thrown about
by the whims of circumstances.

8

Until we start thinking...
Wondering....
Is there more to life?
And begin to seek...

And to ask...
What is the meaning of my life?

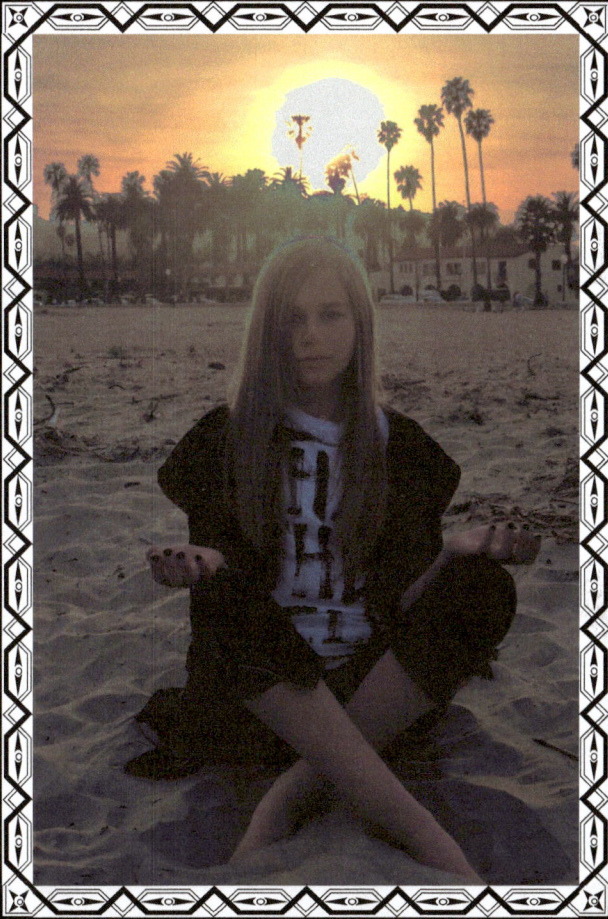

These people
heard the question
and answered
with their actions...

What do you see?
Do you see just animals...?

Or...?

13

Bite an animal.
It'll bite back or flee.

Fight or flight, fight or flight
just a mechanical response.

We're not animals,
we're not machines,
we reject
this mechanical response.

We reject it.
We toss it.
We ignore it.

We turn this cycle
completely around.
Bleep the evil,
change it to good.
If you get bit,
give them food.

A rock acts like a rock.
A dog like a dog.
A child like a child.
A soldier like a soldier.
A saint like a saint.

There is a rock in every one of us.
There is an animal in each one of us.
There is a kid , a killer and a saint
in all of us.

If you're acting in a certain way,

*That is because that is who
you are deep inside.*

Who you are inside,
is how you will act outside.
Change the inside,
and the outside must change.

Take a good look at yourself.
Is your life a knee jerk reaction?

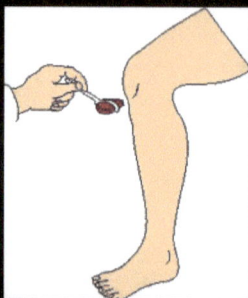

How much of your life
is a conscious
and pre-meditated act?

Animals
are a product
of their circumstances.

You're human.
The circumstances
can be a product of you.

You're a volitional being,
you create the circumstances!

You have free will within!
You refuse to allow the habits
of body and mind to control you.
You are real as a conscious being
because you have inner spiritual
freedom.

Refuse to be a machine-like animal
dominated by the mechanical
functions of your physical body.

Take the spiritual challenge!

The challenge is one that has
stumped many a sleuth.

The age-old question:
How to tame the flesh?

How do I control
my fears and insecurity?
How do I control my anger
and resentment?
How do I control my ego?
How do I keep
from eating
and drinking too much?

Ok, so how?

The grand old traditional way
was to split yourself into two,
the Flesh and the Spirit.
Then you let them fight.

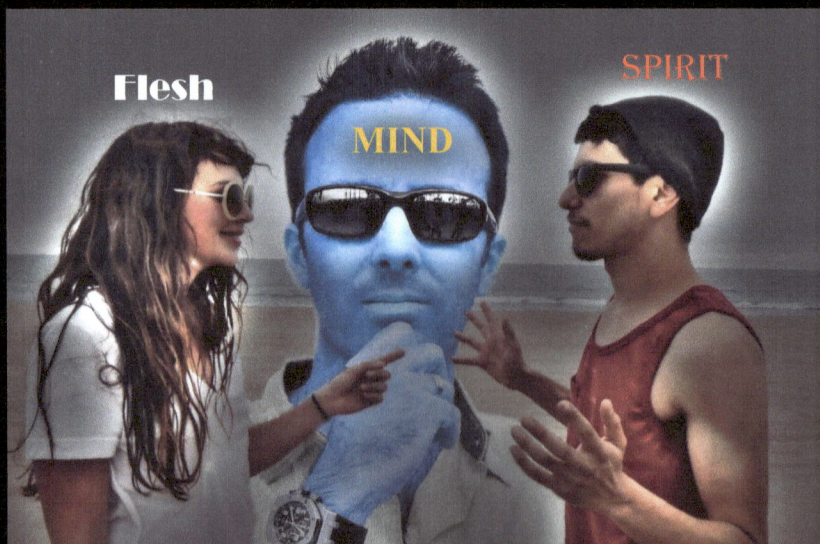

Flesh   MIND   SPIRIT

The mind takes sides
and the battles begin.
Overpower the other side!

Fight! Fight! Fight!

The Flesh wins, the Spirit wins.
the Flesh wins, the Flesh wins, the Flesh
wins, again and again. So you give up.
Because it's too hard.

And it's hard because you are divided.
You lose all your energy fighting
yourself.
How can you accomplish anything with
half your energy?

Let your mind empower your soul,
the flesh and spirit will then become
whole.

The battle within fades,
good actions come naturally.
Moving from your whole self
is the new way!

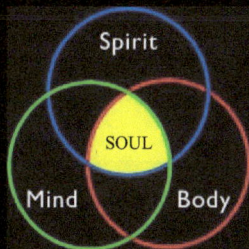

The New Way is to be Whole by Empowering the Soul

Waaaay Old

You split yourself and fight yourself.
You think of your negative aspects as an enemy.
You force yourself through sheer will-power.

New, Cool and Creative

You accept all of yourself as a whole.
You make decisions that pleases the whole, not just your mind, not just your body, not just your spirit, but all three.

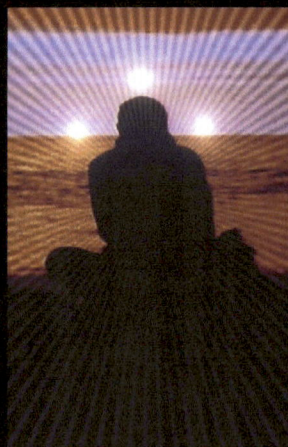

It doesn't mean
that you don't have vices.

It doesn't mean
you don't make mistakes.

It doesn't mean you're perfect.

It means you're okay
with who you are, as you are.

Then, if you really want to change,
you do it without fighting yourself.

You move in the direction
you want to go,
peacefully with no conflict within.
As a whole.

But which part of you will lead?

Who will do the deed?

IS IT YOUR BODY?

Sure, sometimes
you have to allow
the body to lead.

Sometimes, give the wants, desires
and emotions of the body
top priority.

There are things your animal body
needs to do, like eat, play and have sex.
These animal things
are not evil or wrong.
It's just a part of being human,
and a matter of
control and moderation.

But who controls? Who moderates?
Do you control your body
or does your body control you?

Or...

IS IT YOUR MIND?

Let the mind be the master,
sometimes give logic and intellect
the power to lead.

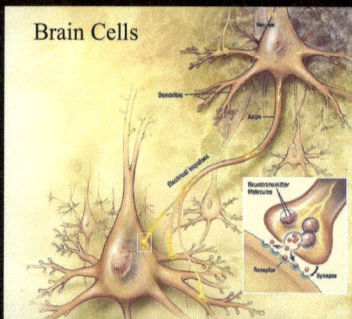

Brain Cells

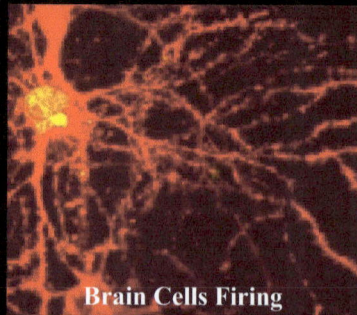

Brain Cells Firing

But mechanical logic
and a cold intellect
lacks love and heart,
and baby's farts,
and humor, magic and fun
which are so desirable
to leading a fulfilling life.

When we are babies
the body is the master.
The body does what it wants;
pee freely, sleep, poop and cry.

As we grow,
the mind becomes our master.
We act out our thoughts.
But the mind is torn
by the wants of the body
and the leadings of the spirit.
Logic and intellect
often can't do the job.

So who?

How About Your Soul?

What is soul?

What is spirit?

Just words.

But they point to something

real within us

that you can feel.

Feel your spirit,
the essence of the Creator
that leads.
Feel your soul,
the essence of you that heeds.

It is the part of you
that knows right from wrong,
good from evil,
beauty from ugliness.

The soul is the best of your body.
The best of your mind.
The best from your spirit.

To truly understand
what the soul is,
you have to feel
your own soul within.

It is the Greatest Love of all.

What is your
Greatest Love within?
What is your greatest desire?

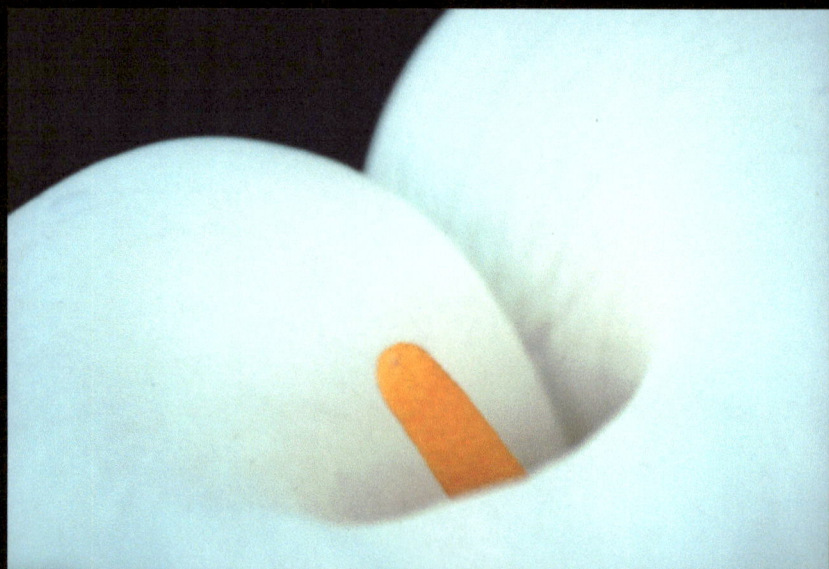

Everything
you are
is because
of this Greatest Love
within
the heart of your heart.

When you were a baby
the greatest desire
may have been for mother's milk.

Then it may have been the desire
to play and have fun.

Then it may have been
wealth and status.

This core value
determines
who you are and how you act.
Some people upgrade
this value only when in crisis.

But when we do it regularly,
purposefully,
we are asserting our volition.

We change the inside
and we change the outside.
But how do we do it, exactly?

AUTHORIZE YOUR SOUL

It has been found
in the halls of neuroscience
a thing called plasticity;
the brain can be molded
by the sparks of mentality.

Worshipful meditation can create
new brain cells and
new connections,
to empower your inner awareness.

You will become aware of your darkness. Don't shrink from it,
look at it unflinchingly, honestly.
Acknowledge it, learn from it,
then move on.

You will become aware of your light. Do right by it. Cherish it and be thankful. Then move on.

This awareness of light and darkness, right and wrong is the
FOUNDATION OF YOUR SOUL.

Meditate on your light, meditate on your darkness. Who are you? Who do you want to be? Really want to be? Way deep inside.

There are many paths, find your own. If you really want it, knock on the door. It's a universal pleasure, not a painful chore!

Reflection and Meditation

Look at your true motivations deep within. Are you satisfied with who you are within? Only you know who you truly are inside. Look.

Do you see the self-centered child within?

Do you see the insecure kid that is afraid to try anything new?

Do you see the spiritual infant crying gimme, gimme, gimme?

But see also
the dynamic young soul within.
This is your true self.

It realizes that you are connected to
everyone, and that you are a valued
member of the universe.
It is this soul that needs
authorization from your mind.

But for your mind to authorize your
soul, your ego has to
change from being a separate part,
to uniting with the Whole.

More is better,
yet less is more.
What is good for you
and yet good for all?

Simply, just allow your soul
to make you whole.
For the soul has a connection to
the divine spark within;
deep inside you
the source of everything.
Love at its purest,
an intelligence all knowing.

Many names there are
for this love intelligence.
The name is not important.
The reality of it is.

The reality is, we draw from this,
all our love, all our energies.

So go deeply.
Touch the Source,
Feel this presence.

Feel it now.

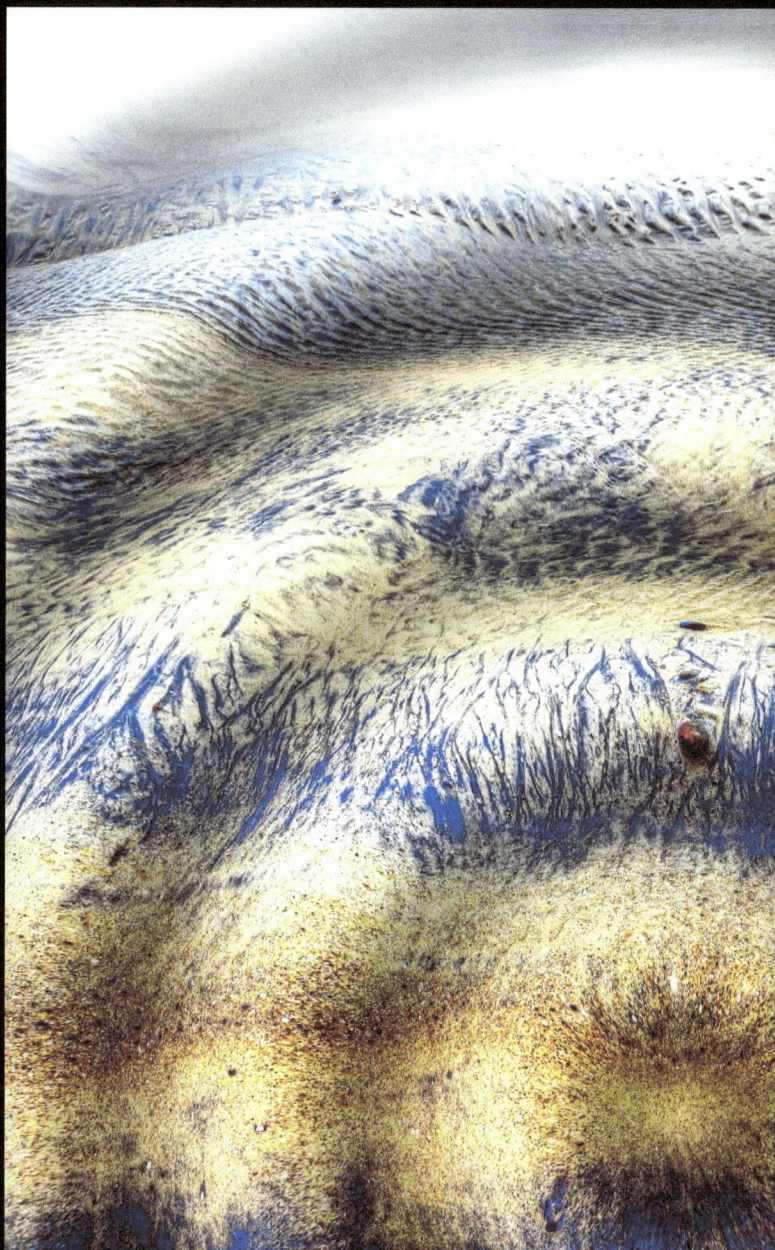

Source

Affirm Deeply

I AM

A Wonderful Being
One And Whole With Source
Healthy and Well
Thankful for My Life

I INTEND

To Give & Receive Unconditional Love
To Reflect Truth, Beauty and Good
To Express My Soul

I ACT

With Mindfulness and Volition
For The Benefit Of All
With Kindness and Love

Your mind
is like a prism.
Your affirmations
the light.

41

In the darkness
A rainbow
Appears in your life.

It Is Done

Your ego relaxes,
and allows your soul
to take the lead,
to achieve wholeness,
your mind acquiesces.
The leadership finally changes,
authority goes to your soul.

42

There is no struggle
like in the days of yore
when battles raged
within your core.
Forget that pattern.
The old way was a chore.
The new way is fun,
relaxing and is a pleasure.
It is the highlight of your day!

The war has ended.
The Flesh and the Spirit are at peace.
You are fully relaxed,
one with your Soul and are whole.
You now realize
the best thing for the universe
is the best thing for you.

43

You are a child
on the shores of infinity.
You are evolving
to a higher state of being.

You manifest
the best of yourself...
you are now
an evolved human.

44

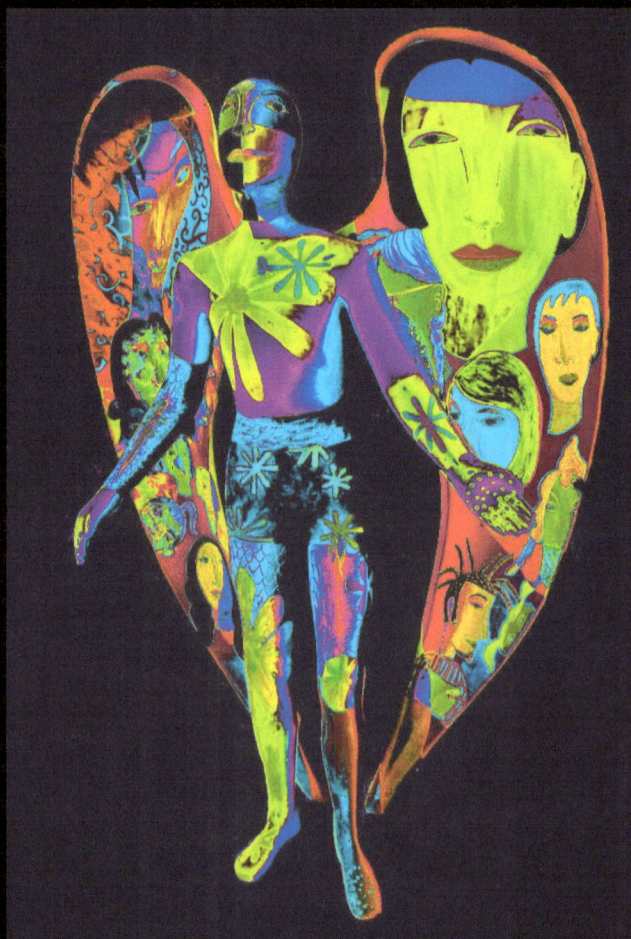

a spiritualized human being...

You are now a Co-Creator
with the Source!

One with the Greatest Love within,
you can now start to manifest this
love in the real world.

You can now re-create your life
according to your inner spiritual
vision.

You were once carried and held by the universal parent.

Now, you can go out on your own, free to explore the true wonders of life!

But now
you've got another challenge.
How are you going to manifest your
creativity?

How do you actually convert
the Greatest Love within
into physical reality?

First of all, don't try too hard.
Remember, you don't want to
fight yourself or force yourself.
Act from your soul,
not for your comfort or ego!

Relax.
Let it come to you.
When you have authorized your
soul, you will start doing the
right things naturally, more and
more without uncertainty. Your
actions will simply be lifted up
by the buoyancy of your soul.

Identify with

transient values

and become

transient.

Identify with

eternal values

and become

eternal.

Keep up your high state of
consciousness.

Cultivate the stillness within.

Therein lies the strength, the love,
the passion, the will, the intent and
desire. You've held it in for so long.

Now, open up,
release the love,
act!

Start by doing those things
that you always knew you should do
but didn't because you were lead by
your body and ego instead of your
soul.

Simple things, like eating more
healthily, exercising, service, reach-
ing out, prayer, meditation, the arts,
be creative!

Since you are now coming from the
soul, all things are do-able. What
was once difficult is now kid's play.

He who hesitates is lost.

Once you have covered the basics,
do things you've never done before!

Conquer your fears!
Challenge your limitations!
Re-create your true self!

Have faith that you can succeed at
doing almost anything!
Reach for the highest goal!

Art by Vince Ventola

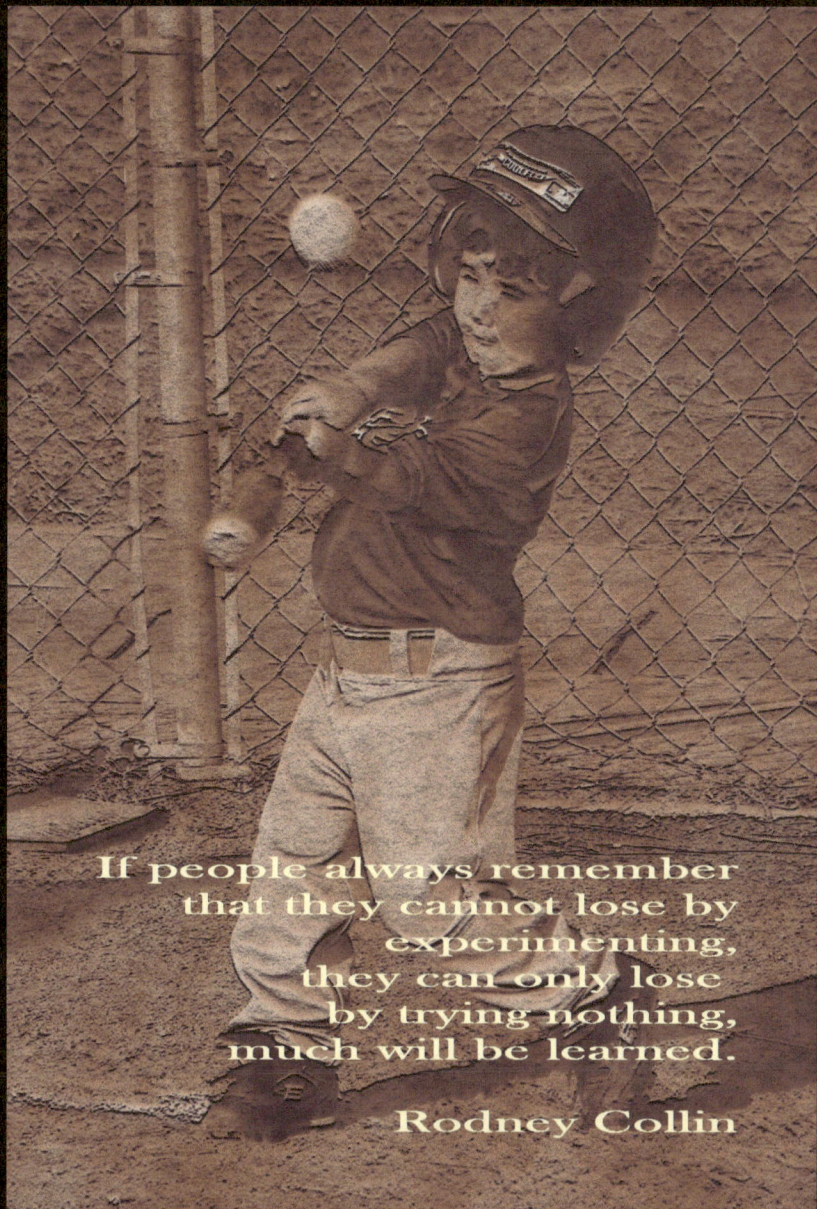

53

If people always remember
that they cannot lose by
experimenting,
they can only lose
by trying nothing,
much will be learned.

Rodney Collin

Atom by atom,
brain cell by brain cell,
service by service,
prayer by prayer,
meditation by meditation,
you evolve.

Your soul leads the way.
You have authorized it.

Peace reigns within.
As a whole person you perceive
the world's true nature.

As the pieces

come together,

you begin to see

a bigger picture...

Our wholeness is Earth's wholeness.

When enough of us authorize our souls,
the Earth, as a whole, becomes truly One
with the universe.

*We are, in reality, evolving
the soul of Earth.*

Together we create Earth's
enlightened consciousness.

For we are the organic part of Earth
that reaches out to the Source.

We have the creative spark
within us.
We have volition.
We are Co-Creators.

The Earth
needs self-awareness
and it starts with you,
right here, right now.

Act on these truths.

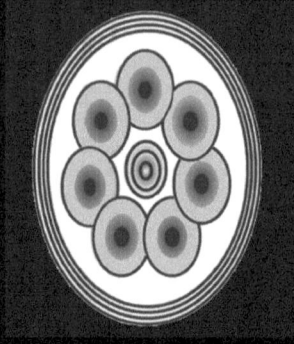

With every revolution
A new iteration.

www.ingramcontent.com/pod-product-compliance
Lightning Source LLC
Chambersburg PA
CBHW040036110426
42741CB00031B/112